CONTENTS

WELCOME TO THE
WORLD OF MINECRAFT 2

WHAT'S NEW IN
MINECRAFT? 4

CAVES & CLIFFS
MOBS...........................6

CAVES & CLIFFS
ITEMS........................8

CAVES & CLIFFS
BLOCKS.....................10

CAVES & CLIFFS
BIOMES.....................12

QUICK BUILD 1
TREEHOUSE BASE...........16

TOP 10 MOST
DANGEROUS MOBS..........18

REDSTONE GUIDE...........20

TOP 10 BEST
MINECRAFT SKINS 22

QUICK BUILD 2
TNT LAUNCHER 24

TOP 10 THINGS
TO TRY
IN MINECRAFT 26

MOST POWERFUL
MINECRAFT WEAPONS...28

HIDDEN SECRETS 30

QUICK BUILD 3
AUTOMATIC STORAGE
SYSTEM.....................32

THE NETHER GUIDE 34

THE END GUIDE 36

TOP 10
POTIONS 38

BEST FREE
MINECRAFT MAPS 40

OCEAN GUIDE 42

TOP 10
EPIC BUILDS.................46

MINECRAFT'S
BIG NUMBERS...............48

LittleBrother
BOOKS

Published 2022
Little Brother Books Ltd, Ground Floor,
23 Southernhay East, Exeter, Devon, EX1 1QL
Printed in the United Kingdom
books@littlebrotherbooks.co.uk
www.littlebrotherbooks.co.uk

The Little Brother Books trademarks, logos, email and website addresses and
the Games Warrior logo and imprint are sole and exclusive properties of Little
Brother Books Limited.

KU-215-378

WELCOME TO THE WORLD OF MINECRAFT

Mojang's Minecraft is one of the biggest video games in the world and it just keeps on growing. Grab your pickaxe and get ready to start your own blocky adventures!

GETTING STARTED

Players begin their Minecraft journey by choosing what their character will look like. Tweak your avatar's hair, face, clothing, feet and much more.

GAME MODES

To start a game, you'll need to choose from different game types. In Single player you select Survival or Creative modes, depending on what you want to try.

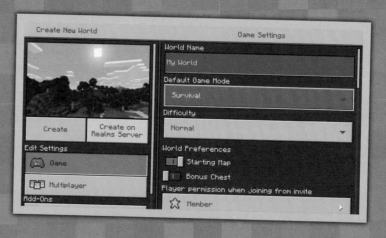

SURVIVAL MODE

In Survival you'll need to craft items, hunt for food and supplies, battle hostile mobs and try to make it through each day in one piece. Are you up for the challenge?

CREATIVE MODE

In this mode, the sky's the limit! You'll have access to every single items in the game and can build anything that your imagination can come up with.

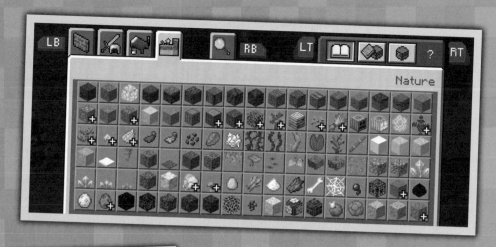

MULTIPLAYER

If you want to play online with your friends, then you'll need to either set up a server or join one that's already been created. Multiplayer Minecraft is lots of fun!

MINECRAFT REALMS PLUS

Take your gaming to the next level with Minecraft Realms Plus. This £7.99 per month subscription service lets you try out all kinds of new features.

BUILDING AND EXPLORING

To become a true Minecraft expert, you'll need to explore every biome (or world) that you can and build everything you can possibly think of.

There's always something new to see and do in Minecraft and this Ultimate Guide is packed with hints, tips and ideas to help you get started on your journey!

WHAT'S NEW IN MINECRAFT?

CAVES & CLIFFS

Minecraft received two major updates in 2021 with Caves & Cliffs. New biomes, features, mobs and items were added to the game and well-received by fans.

MINECRAFT PREVIEW

Players can now try out new Bedrock Edition game features with Minecraft Preview. This is currently only available on iOS, Android and Windows devices.

EXPERIMENTAL FEATURES

With update 1.18.10 Mojang has also added lots of Experimental Features that include new frogs and tadpole mobs, as well as decorative skulk blocks.

MINECRAFT X PUMA

In early 2022, Minecraft teamed up with sportswear brand PUMA to release a cool clothing collection. You can pick up trainers, T-shirts, hoodies and more.

There's always something new to see, do and build in the world of Minecraft! Here's what's been going on in Mojang Studios' blocky universe recently...

ONE TRILLION VIEWS

Minecraft reached another amazing milestone in 2021 when its official YouTube channel hit 1,000,000,000,000 views over the last 10 years. That's amazing!

MINECRAFT LIVE 2021

At the annual Minecraft Live 2021 event, Mojang revealed there would be major additions coming to the game in 2022 with the highly-anticipated The Wild Update.

WHAT'S IN THE WILD?

The Wild Update is set to include brand-new blocks and mobs, Deep Dark City and Mangrove swamp biomes, plus the deadly Warden mob. He looks spooky!

MINECRAFT NOW

In late 2021, Mojang announced a new series on its YouTube channel. Minecraft Now lets players watch the game's developers talk about what they're working on.

CAVES & CLIFFS MOBS

AXOLOTL

Based on real-life endangered Mexican salamanders, these strange amphibians can often be found in bodies of water located within lush cave biomes.

There are four common varieties of axolotl in Minecraft, lucy (pink), wild (brown), gold and cyan, plus a rare blue version with a 0.08334 chance of spawning.

When damaged an axolotl will play dead, but slowly regenerate its health, just as the real-life amphibian can regrow its lost limbs!

Tempt an axolotl with a tropical fish and it will attack fish, glow squid, squid, drowned and guardians (but not Elder Guardians) for you.

GOAT

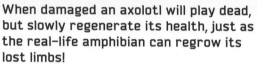

Of the three new Mobs added in the Cliffs & Caves updates, goats are the only neutral ones. They spawn in mountain biomes.

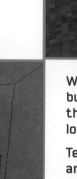

Goats can jump very high! When attacked or threatened, they can leap up to five blocks to get away from enemies.

Mobs attacked by goats won't ever attack them back. Goats also won't bother battling ghasts or other goats, which is odd...

It's possible for goats to be bred using wheat, which produces a baby goat. When they ram into a block, goats will drop a goat horn item.

With the latest updates to Minecraft come three amazing new mobs that can be encountered and interacted with. How many have you seen so far?

GLOW SQUID

Based on the basic squid mob of the same name from Minecraft Earth, glow squid can spawn in any underwater biome location.

When you attack and defeat a glow squid, it will drop glow ink sacs. These can be added to signs and item frames to make them glow.

After taking some damage, a glow squid will stop glowing and swim away. The light level in a biome isn't affected by how bright a glow squid is.

Glow squids were added to the game after a successful fan vote. The other potential mobs that might have been added were the Moonbloom and Iceologer.

CAVES & CLIFFS ITEMS

AMETHYST SHARD

These crystal pieces are dropped from smashed amethyst clusters. They can be used to make spyglasses and tinted glass.

BUCKET OF AXOLOTL

Use a water bucket on an axolotl and you can then use this item to spawn a water block with the mob inside it. That's crazy!

COPPER INGOT

Smelt raw copper and you'll create a copper ingot. This can be used to craft copper blocks, lightning rods and spyglasses.

GLOW BERRIES

You can find this tasty fruit growing from cave vines. It can be eaten, used as a light source and is loved by foxes!

GLOW INK SAC

Dropped by a glow squid when it's attacked. They can be added to signs and items frames to make them glow in the dark.

There are all kinds of fascinating new items to find and use in the game. Try collecting as many of these as you can and see what they do!

RAW IRON, GOLD AND COPPER

Found by mining ore blocks, these metals can be smelted into ingots for crafting. Use the Fortune Enchantment to get more iron and gold.

POWDER SNOW BUCKET

Take a bucket and use it on snow powder to create this item. You can then use it to place powder snow wherever you like.

SPAWN EGGS

The latest game update has now added spawn eggs for the three new mobs (see p6-7): axolotl, glow squid and goat.

SPYGLASS

Crafted from an amethyst shard and two copper ingots. Allows players to see objects from very far away.

MUSIC DISC

The new music disc from music composer Lena Rane, titled 'Otherside', can be found in some stronghold and dungeon chests.

CAVES & CLIFFS BLOCKS

There are all kinds of interesting new types of blocks to play around with in the latest updates, letting players create all sorts of incredible builds.

AZALEA LEAVES

Part of the new azalea tree, marking the location of a lush cave.

AMETHYST

Crafted with four amethyst shards. Makes a tinkling sound when walked on.

CALCITE

Can generate in stony peaks. Spawns between smooth basalt and amethyst.

COPPER BLOCK

Used for crafting and storage. Made with nine copper ingots.

COPPER ORE

Found underground in ore veins. Drops raw copper when broken.

DEEPSLATE

Can be found below level coordinates Y = 0. Takes twice as long to mine as normal stone.

DRIPSTONE BLOCK

Spawns in dripstone caves. Crafted from four-pointed dripstone.

GLOW LICHEN

Looks similar to vines. Spreads to blocks when bone meal is used on it.

MOSS BLOCK

Use bone meal to make this block grow grass, tall grass and moss carpets.

POWDER SNOW

Enemies can fall through this block and take freezing damage.

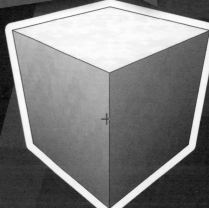

ROOTED DIRT

Part of the azalea plant. The first roots that have existed in the game.

SMOOTH BASALT

Looks similar to calcite. Obtained by smelting basalt in a furnace.

TINTED GLASS

A type of glass that doesn't allow light to pass through it.

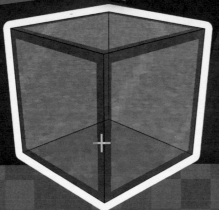

TUFF

A grey block formed from volcanic ash. Can be used for decoration.

CAVES & CLIFFS BIOMES

DRIPSTONE CAVES

With mining being such a huge part of the game, it makes sense that Mojang would want to head back underground for a new spin on classic biomes. This new location is filled with clusters and pillars of pointed dripstone and dripstone blocks.

As you explore these new caves, you'll encounter stalactites hanging from above and stalagmites growing from the ground. There are also lots of small water wells made up from 1x1 blocks that can come in handy.

One of the main reasons to check out the dripstone caves is the huge amount of copper ore that you'll find down there. Mine these to make copper ingots and blocks, which can then be used for crafting all sorts of cool items.

Large copper and iron veins can also be seen snaking through these caves. They're easy to spot, as they're usually all over the floors, walls and ceilings, so there is definitely plenty of material to be mined.

LUSH CAVES

Unlike the fairly empty dripstone caves, lush caves are filled with all kinds of plants and vegetation. Found underground below azalea trees, these areas are amazing to explore and have a variety of mobs living in them.

As well as bats, glow squid and tropical fish, lush caves are also home to axolotls, which are exclusive to this biome. However, keep your eyes open as you will also bump into spiders, creepers, witches and skeletons!

Moss, grass and azalea bushes can be found on the floor and ceiling, with vines growing glow berries on them. You'll also encounter springs and shallow lakes, where you can find clay and dripleaf plants.

If you're very lucky, you may discover large amethyst geodes underground, which have cracked open to reveal shiny purple crystals inside. You'll also sometimes see these on beaches and underwater.

One of the biggest changes to Minecraft in the latest game updates are the addition of some all-new and exciting biomes to explore: Caves & Cliffs!

MOUNTAINS

Head higher up into the new Minecraft biomes and you'll scale the heights of all-new mountains. From towering peaks and snow-covered crags, there are six sub-biomes just waiting to be climbed.

MEADOW

Similar to the plains, this new biome is filled with grassy open spaces, flowers and tall grass. Here you're guaranteed to encounter all kinds of passive mobs such as sheep, donkeys and rabbits.

There are both pillager outposts and plains villages to explore, making it the only mountain biome where those villages can generate. This biome is usually found on the lower sides of some mountains.

GROVE

Start heading up a mountain slope and you'll enter the grove at much higher altitudes. This wintery biome features thick forests of spruce trees, with the ground covered in a light dusting of powder snow.

Rabbits, wolves and red foxes all spawn here, although it's often hard to spot them hiding in the forests. There are all kinds of blocks to be mined in the grove such as emerald ore, infested stone and spruce logs.

SNOWY SLOPES

This cold biome is mostly barren and covered in a thick layer of snow. Watch out for the long drops off towering stone cliffs and see if you can spot an igloo, the only biome where they generate.

Snowy slopes are also home to rabbits and one of the game's new mobs, goats. Make sure you don't annoy them too much though, as they're likely to give you a nasty headbutt which will send you flying!

JAGGED PEAKS

One of three peak biomes, jagged peaks feature very tall mountains, with some being so high that the tops of them are above the clouds. A single layer of snow covers stone, slopes and huge cliffs.

Due to the high terrain and cold conditions, the only passive mob to spawn here are goats. Start mining for ores in this biome and you'll discover rich seams of coal, iron, infested stone and emerald.

FROZEN PEAKS

This is another wintery biome that's covered in powder snow, snow blocks and massive glaciers of packed ice. This biome generates in smaller and smoother hills, as well as in slightly jagged peaks.

Explore this frozen biome and you'll encounter remote and rare pillage outposts, which can be visited or attacked. As with jagged peaks, the only passive mob that spawn in this hostile environment are goats.

STONY PEAKS

This biome is a warmer variation of both jagged peaks and frozen peaks. It generates in warm biomes such as savannas and jungles and is mostly covered in stone and large strips of calcite.

All of the plants in this biome have a special light green colour to them, making them look really unique. Dig underground and you'll soon find plenty of calcite, infested stone and emerald ore.

TREEHOUSE BASE

Take a look at the first of our awesome Minecraft Quick Build guides. We'll teach you how to get started in the game by making this awesome Treehouse Base!

1

Begin by selecting Creative mode and starting a new game. Next, take a look around the biome, find a suitable tree and then lay down some birch wood planks.

Dark Oak Wood Planks

2

Around the main section of the floor, start adding some dark oak wood planks. This makes the level bigger and looks great when paired with the birch wood.

3

With your floor in place, start building up the walls of the treehouse using dark oak wood planks all around the outside. The walls can be as high as you like.

4

The walls in this treehouse build are 3 x blocks high. Don't forget to leave some holes in the blocks for a door and as many windows as you might want.

5

Here's how the treehouse is looking from the inside. Once you've finished the main build, you can add all kinds of furniture and decorations to the interior.

6

Now place simple glass panes into each window section, then head to the front of the house to add a door. We've gone for a simple jungle wood door.

7

For a fun looking roof, head to the top of your treehouse and place hay bales in a small pyramid shape. These are a great colour and really make your base stand out.

8

For a finishing touch, lay down lots of jungle trapdoors all over the hay bales. With your Treehouse Base completed, all you need to do is invite your friends over!

TOP 10 MOST DANGEROUS MOBS

GHAST

The second-largest mob in Minecraft, the Nether's spookiest resident can shoot highly-explosive fireballs that cause massive damage to whatever they touch.

DROWNED

These underwater zombies can be real trouble if there are a lot of them near you, but grab a trident and you'll make quick work of this aquatic mob.

GUARDIANS

Both guardians and elder guardians have lethal lasers that can't be dodged. If you see any spawning near ocean monuments, hit them hard and fast.

ENDERMEN

Probably the spookiest mob in the game, endermen exist in the End and will only turn hostile if you attack them first or get too close.

VEXES

These mobs are summoned by evokers and are basically illagers with wings. They can phase through blocks and attack with sharp swords.

There are all kinds of dangerous creatures lurking in Minecraft, so you need to keep a look out for them at all times. But which mobs are the most dangerous?

PHANTOMS

If you don't manage to sleep for three or more days in Minecraft, then phantoms will spawn in groups of six and launch at you. Yikes!

BABY ZOMBIES

This mob might look cute, but don't let that fool you. Baby zombies are much faster than the bigger versions and can swarm you in seconds.

BEES

They might be small, but this mob can be lethal! If you bother them or go near their nests, they'll sting you with a nasty poison.

WITHER

A three-headed mob from the Nether, withers are deadly. They can cause huge explosions and are immune to fire, lava and drowning damage.

ENDER DRAGON

The final boss in single player Survival mode, this hostile mob is very tough to beat. Defeat it and you'll get 12,000 XP and a rare dragon egg.

REDSTONE GUIDE

REDSTONE BLOCKS

Redstone exists as an ore that will first need to be mined. Once you've broken them down you can use redstone dust to make redstone circuits that connect to your builds.

POWERED-UP

There are no electronics in Minecraft, so redstone takes its place. With a redstone circuit in place, you'll also need a suitable power source to get things going.

LEVERS, BUTTONS AND TORCHES

All of these items can provide a redstone signal. They can be always on or be switches that are activated by players. Levers, buttons and torches have basic on/off functions.

POWERED BLOCKS

Many types of blocks can be powered if they're attached to a power source. A powered block can be used to switch on the block placed next to it. These blocks can be powered:

All stone and brick blocks
Wood and wool

Dirt, grass, gravel and sand
Double slabs

Droppers and dispensers

REDSTONE DUST

Placing a line of redstone dust along objects makes a wire that connects blocks, power sources and devices. When powered, the dust lights up and sparkles.

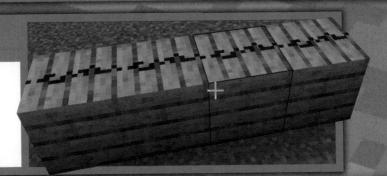

To become a real Minecraft pro, you'll need to master the art of using redstone. This special material can power all sorts of creations, so let's find out how to get started!

POWER DISTANCE

The power from redstone dust only travels one block's length. You'll need to add more dust to connect multiple blocks and keep the juice flowing.

REDSTONE REPEATERS

To extend the signal strength of the power source, you'll need to add a redstone repeater. These items have multiple switches to boost and add delays to power.

REDSTONE DEVICES

There are lots of simple devices you can try building, such as doors, gates, redstone lamps and pistons. Just remember your redstone dust and power supply.

DROPPERS AND DISPENSERS

These are really handy devices that can hold nine stacks of items and then release them one at a time when they receive a redstone signal.

REDSTONE CRAFTING

Once you get the hang of adding redstone to your builds, you'll be able to make all kinds of amazing mechanisms and machines, from pistons to elevators and more!

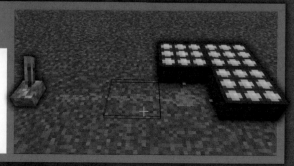

TOP 10 BEST MINECRAFT SKINS

AMONG US

Fresh from Innersloth's super-popular multiplayer game, these mysterious astronaut skins are available in purple, brown, cyan and lime green.

IRON MAN

Tony Stark's armoured alter ego gets his very own Minecraft skin and it's really great. Make your avatar look just like Iron Man does in the Marvel movies!

SANTA HD

Now you can play as Santa Claus all year round! This HD version of Father Christmas is very detailed and perfect for playing with in snowy biomes.

ASH KETCHUM

Show all of your friends just how huge a Pokémon fan you are by wearing the iconic baseball cap, waistcoat and gloves of this master catcher.

PANDA

This adorable Minecraft skin is quite simple, but adorable. Head on over to a biome with plenty of tasty bamboo and you'll be in panda heaven.

You can buy all sorts of amazing items from the Minecraft Avatar Shop and then use them to customise your character. Check out this list of the top 10 favourited items in the Shop, as voted for by players from all around the world!

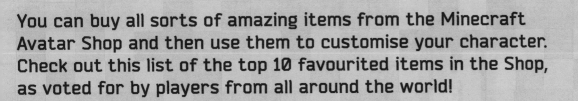

UNICORN

Now you may not believe in unicorns, but add this rainbow onesie to a blonde-haired girl character and you might just change your mind.

TETRIS

A classic video game spawns a classic Minecraft skin. Looking like some sort of crazy supervillain outfit, the Tetris skin is definitely one-of-a-kind.

CREEPER

Really confuse your friends with your very own Creeper skin! However, it won't fool the real thing, so keep your eyes peeled for the green mobs.

HEROBRINE

A legendary character some players say is hidden within Minecraft's code, Herorbine is rumoured to be the ghost of Notch's dead brother...

OVER WORLD

Guaranteed to help you blend into your environment, the Over World skin's biome background pattern makes it the perfect camouflage for hiding from other players.

2 TNT LAUNCHER

1 Begin by finding a flat open space to work on. If there are trees, rocks or other objects in the way, just clear them out until you have room to get started.

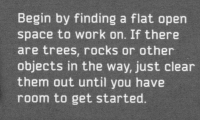

2 Now make a basic frame of 12 dispensers facing in towards each other. In the centre of this area, place a 3x3 grid made up of smooth stone blocks.

Oak Fence

3 Position one oak fence piece on the middle smooth stone block. Carefully pour water into just the top corner of the build and then the bottom corner.

4 With the water in place, add 24 smooth stone blocks all around the base. On top of these blocks you'll need to add redstone dust all the way around.

For the second Quick Build, take a look at how to make this incredible TNT Launcher. This is a great mechanism to create and one that will totally amaze your friends!

5 On top of one of the middle dispensers, place a smooth stone block. Then take an oak button and position that on top of the block.

6 Next you'll need to grab plenty of TNT and fill up each of the dispensers in the frame. They all need to contain the same amount of the explosive block.

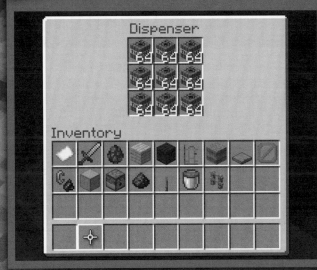

7 As a fun touch (and to let other players know to keep their distance), try making a giant warning sign next to the frame, made from yellow and black concrete blocks.

8 Finally, just stand on the oak fence piece, press the button and wait for a massive TNT explosion to launch you way up into the sky! How far do you think you can you leap?

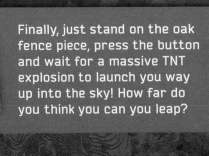

TOP 10 THINGS TO TRY IN MINECRAFT

COMPLETE ACHIEVEMENTS

There are so many achievements to get in Minecraft that it will take ages to tick them all off. Try getting a full set of netherite armour or defeating a wither.

COBBLESTONE GENERATOR

Dig a 1x3 block hole in the ground, put lava in one end and water in the other and you'll make yourself an endless supply of cobblestone.

SLAY THE ENDER DRAGON

Grab a diamond sword and armour, lots of potions and golden apples and then go slay the biggest creature in the whole of Minecraft!

FIND AXOLOTLS

This new Caves & Cliffs update mob spawns in five different colours and are found on lush cave biomes. Can you find the super-rare blue version?

HUNT FOR RARE ITEMS

After defeating the Ender Dragon, search the End Islands for a city with a ship and you should pick up the Elytra, which allows you to fly.

Minecraft is a game with unlimited possibilities, but if you're ever bored and looking for a new challenge, check out this list of top 10 things to try out!

TRY NEW FEATURES

There are so many cool features in the Caves & Cliffs update. Try out as many as you can, such as making a spyglass or finding amethyst geodes.

MINE FOR DIAMONDS

Usually found underground in layers 5-12, diamonds are one of the toughest items in the game, allowing you to craft all kinds of stuff.

PLAY WITH FRIENDS

Whilst exploring new biomes is fun, it's more enjoyable with someone else. Play online with your friends and try building something amazing together!

BLOW UP A TNT PYRAMID

Try stacking as much TNT together as you can, then hitting it and standing well back. The more impressive and bigger the explosion the better.

MAKE A TREEHOUSE

Try building your own private den in a jungle biome. Decorate it with whatever items you like, then invite your friends to come and visit!

MOST POWERFUL MINECRAFT WEAPONS

TNT

You might not think of TNT as a weapon, but it can cause massive amounts of damage. However, TNT can also blow you up too, so be careful when using it!

SPLASH POTIONS

There are two splash potions that can make a big difference in mob fights: poison and weakness. Make them on a brewing stand and you'll be ready for any battle.

IRON SWORD

This is quite an easy weapon to craft and it's also one that does a decent amount of damage. You just need two iron ingots and a stick to craft it.

STONE AXE

A stone axe will actually deal as much damage as iron and diamond axes. Craft your simple weapon using three stone blocks and two sticks.

BOW

To strike enemies from a safe distance, you'll definitely need a bow. This weapon can be crafted from three strings, which are dropped by skeletons, and three sticks.

The biomes in Minecraft can be very dangerous, so you'll need to be able to defend yourself. Take a look at our list of the most powerful weapons to have in the game.

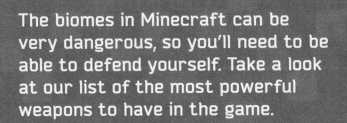

DIAMOND SWORD

Although diamonds are hard to find, they're worth it for a diamond sword. Use sharpness and fire aspect enchantments on the sword and it'll be pretty unbeatable.

CROSSBOW

This is a really overpowered weapon! Crossbows can be loaded with arrows or fireworks too. Craft using three sticks, two strings, an iron ingot and a tripwire hook.

NETHERITE AXE

Dealing 10 damage, the netherite axe is very powerful. Place a diamond axe and a netherite ingot on a smithing table to craft this truly formidable weapon.

TRIDENT

You only have a 15% chance of a drowned dropping this weapon, but it's worth it. There's no way to craft a trident in Minecraft, so grab one when you can.

NETHERITE SWORD

Crafted from a diamond sword and a netherite ingot on a smithing table. Try different enchantments on it and you'll have the most powerful weapon in the game!

HIDDEN SECRETS

MOOSHROOM

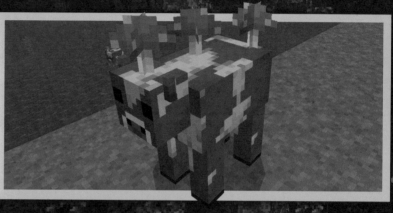

The rare Mooshroom only spawns on the Mushroom Island biome. Using a wooden bowl, it's actually possible to milk these red and white cows and get an unlimited supply of tasty mushroom soup!

UPSIDE DOWN

Try turning mobs upside down! All you have to do is place an egg on an anvil and then rename it 'Dinnerbone". Now simply spawn as many of the mobs as you like and they will all be the other way up.

PUMPKIN HEAD

If you're being overwhelmed by hordes of endermen, simply place a pumpkin on your head and they won't react to you. Also try switching to the first person view to look out of the eye holes!

PINK SHEEP

Did you know that pink sheep do appear in Minecraft? These super-rare animals have a legendary status, with a 0.01% chance of spawning and the baby version is even rarer with a 0.0082% spawn chance.

Do you think you have what it takes to be a Minecraft pro? Check out these awesome Minecraft secrets and see how many you've managed to find in the game so far.

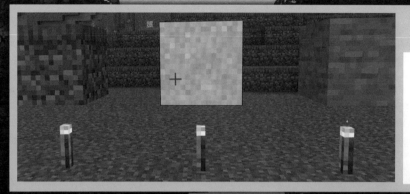

TORCHES

Torches are actually super strong! Place a flaming torch on a wall or floor, then put any type and number of solid blocks on top. The torches will support the blocks, no matter what substance they're made from.

COLLAR COLOUR

Dogs are easily one of the best animals in Minecraft. If you have a dog that you've tamed, you can use any of the 16 possible dyes in the game to change the colour of your canine's collar.

CATS VS CREEPERS

Creepers are one of the deadliest foes in the game and best avoided. Most mobs and players avoid them, but their biggest enemies are cats! Load your home up with lots of feline friends to protect it.

ZOMBIE CURE

Villagers sometimes get zombified, but it is possible to cure them. You'll need to make a Splash Potion of Weakness, throw it at the zombified villager, then use a golden apple on it.

Splash Potion of Weakness
Weakness (3:00)

AUTOMATIC STORAGE SYSTEM

1
Before you can begin your next creation you'll need to find or clear away a decent amount of working space. Make sure the ground is nice and flat for this build.

2
Next, begin by placing nine large chests next to and on top of each other to form the pattern as shown below. Make sure they're stacked as closely as possible.

3
Now start to add stone brick blocks around the side, back and in front of the chests. Note that some of these will be removed later on in the build.

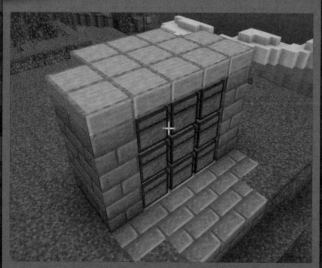

4
Over the top of the stone brick blocks and chests you'll need to add a series of smooth stone slabs. You'll need 10 in total to cover over the top of them.

The final Quick Build might seem a little more complicated, but it's actually quite simple. Follow the steps below and make your own Automatic Storage System!

Head round to the back of the build and add nine hoppers underneath the overhanging smooth stone slabs. These should be stacked in a 3x3 grid formation.

Place glass blocks over the top and down one side. Add one hopper in the floor as shown, with no glass above it. Leave a centre channel empty on top and fill it with water.

Add in more dispensers round the back of your creation, on top of the existing ones. You'll also need to place one last glass block to stop the water escaping.

Finally, add a lever to the hopper. Drop items into the hopper, hit the switch and they'll travel up, through the water and be automatically sorted into the chests!

THE NETHER GUIDE

CREATING A NETHER PORTAL

To access this location, players will need to make a Nether portal. You'll need to build a rectangular obsidian frame and then activate it with fire.

ENTERING THE NETHER

Stepping inside the portal will instantly transport you to the Nether. This dimension is dark and menacing, filled with fire, lava hostile mobs and unique structures.

GLOOMY WORLD

The Nether is mostly made from bedrock blocks and has no daylight or weather. Light in this gloomy world comes from fire, lava, portals, shroomlights and glowstone.

NETHER BIOMES

As with the Overworld, the Nether features a number of different biomes: Nether Wastes, Crimson Forest, Warped Forest, Soul Sand Valley and Basalt Delta.

When you're ready for a real challenge in Minecraft, head into the dark and dangerous dimension known as the Nether. Will you survive the experience?

START EXPLORING

Start exploring the Nether and you'll discover strange structures such as Nether fortresses, bastion remnants, ruined portals and Nether fossils.

DANGEROUS MOBS

Some of the most dangerous mobs in Minecraft exist within the Nether. Keep your eyes open for Magma Cubes, Endermen, Piglins, Skeletons, Ghast and worse!

SPECIAL ITEMS

One good excuse to journey to the Nether is to mine special items and blocks. These include Nether quartz ore, Nether wart, soul sand and magma blocks.

STRANGE THINGS

Very strange things happen in the Nether. Beds explode, water doesn't exist, clocks spin wildly and lava flows twice as far and six times faster than in the Overworld.

THE END GUIDE

THIS IS THE END

A space-like alternate dimension, the End consists of a number of islands and structures floating in the void that are made out of end stone.

THE EYES OF ENDER

To access the End, players need eyes of ender to find a stronghold that has an End portal. Placing 12 eyes of ender into the portal frames activates it.

ENDERMEN

As in the Nether, there's no day or night, nor is there any weather. In fact, it never rains in the Nether as this would damage Endermen.

BIOMES

The End is made up of five different and varied biomes: The End, Small End Islands, End Midlands, End Highlands and End Barrens.

The final challenge in Minecraft will test even the most experienced pro players. Armour up, grab your best potions and weapons and prepare to journey to... the End!

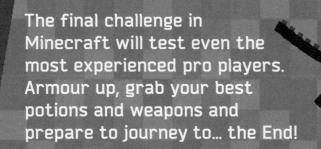

STRUCTURES

There are a number of different structures in the End that include the End spike, obsidian platform, End gateway, End City, chorus tree and End ship.

EXPLORE

Be sure to thoroughly explore every End ship. These are the only locations where you'll find the rare elytra wings and dragon head items.

MOBS

Three mobs exist in the End and they're all deadly. The ominous Endermen, the fast-moving Shulkers and the game's final challenge, the Ender dragon!

THE ENDER DRAGON

To beat the Ender dragon, players need to destroy the End crystals it uses to regenerate, then take down the beast using distance weapons. Good luck!

TOP 10 POTIONS

1

SLOW FALLING

If you want to avoid taking massive damage or dying from a fall, then this is the potion for you. You'll need a water bottle, nether wart and a Phantom Membrane.

2

INVISIBILITY

A powerful potion, Invisibility is quite expensive to make and also wears off. To make it you'll first need to make a Potion of Night Vision then add a fermented spider eye.

3

LEAPING

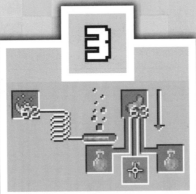

To reach higher places much easier, just brew up a handy Potion of Leaping. You can make it from a water bottle, nether wart and rabbit's foot combined.

4

SWIFTNESS

Make an Awkward Potion using a water bottle, nether wart and blaze powder. Now add some sugar from farming sugarcane to finish.

Potions are incredibly useful items that can be created using a brewing stand. By combining different items, it's possible to make potions that give you amazing abilities and can even save your life!

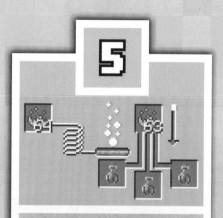

STRENGTH

To cause plenty of damage to your enemies, brew up a batch of this potion. It's easy to make using a water bottle, nether wart and blaze powder.

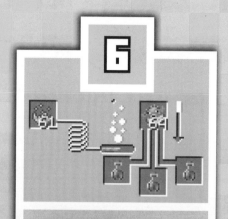

WATER BREATHING

Make an Awkward Potion using a water bottle, nether wart and blaze powder. Then add a Puffer Fish and your potion will be ready.

NIGHT VISION

Brew an Awkward Potion using a water bottle, nether wart and blaze powder. To finish it off, throw in a golden carrot and you're all done.

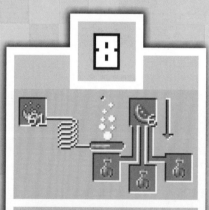

HEALING

Extra health during battles can always come in handy. To make a Potion of Healing, combine a water bottle, nether wart and a glistering melon.

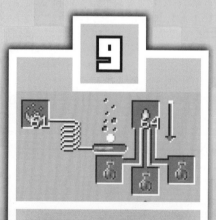

REGENERATION

Make an Awkward Potion using a water bottle, nether wart and blaze powder. Now add a rare Ghast Tear to complete the process.

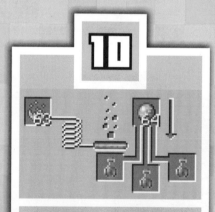

FIRE RESISTANCE

Create an Awkward Potion using a water bottle, nether wart and blaze powder. Add magma cream to the brew and it's ready to go.

BEST FREE MINECRAFT MAPS

10 YEARS OF MINECRAFT

To celebrate the 10th anniversary of Minecraft, Blockworks released this tribute map that takes you on a tour through the history of the game.

TERRA SWOOP FORCE

Travel to the core of the world with the Elytra adventure map from Noxcrew featuring explosive cave action and fully-voiced characters.

FARM LIFE

This is an awesome farming simulator from PixelHeads. Drive tractors, plant crops, look after animals and breed new mobs.

SAFARI WORLD

Take on the role of a wildlife photographer and take pictures of amazing animals in this huge map from Cyclone Designs.

ASTRONAUT TRAINING CENTER

Ever wanted to travel into space? Here's your chance! Train to be an astronaut, learn about the universe and prepare for blast off.

If you're looking for some inspiration for your own world creations or just want to check out what other players have been building, download any of these free Minecraft maps for an awesome adventure!

BLOOM

This is a very calm and relaxing map that lets you look after an abandoned garden and grow over 30 different magical plants.

CAVES & CLIFFS EXPLORERS

From creators Spark Universe, this awesome map guides you through the latest game update with lots of fun quests.

GRAVE DANGER

Help protect a castle from hordes of undead monsters! Use traps, magical weapons and your trusty companion to save the day.

INTERNATIONAL SPACE STATION

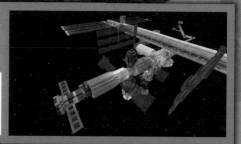

Created by Minecraft and NASA, this adventure map lets you experience life on the actual International Space Station.

MARINE BIOLOGIST ROLEPLAY

Dive into the ocean as a marine biologist to encounter 20 aquatic animals, a drivable submarine, aquarium and more.

OCEAN GUIDE

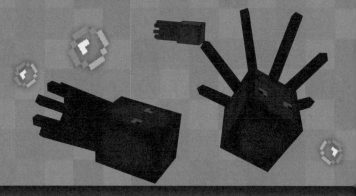

AQUATIC BIOMES

Oceans are aquatic biomes and the largest type in Minecraft. They can cover around 25–33% of the surface area of the overworld and are often very deep.

SURVIVAL MODE

Travelling underwater in survival mode requires an air supply. You can use a potion of water breathing, wear a turtle shell or make a conduit to transport oxygen.

SEEING UNDERWATER

Making a potion of night vision is a good idea, as it will help you see underwater. You'll need a water bottle, nether wart and golden carrot.

OCEAN BIOMES

There are nine different oceans biomes in Minecraft: Ocean, Deep, Frozen, Deep Frozen, Cold, Deep Cold, Lukewarm, Deep Lukewarm and Warm.

The oceans in Minecraft are great fun to explore and there are all kinds of hidden treasures just waiting to be discovered. Get ready to plunge into the murky depths!

CRAFTING A BOAT

Crafting a boat is the best way to travel over the ocean. Not only will it increase your speed, it will also save you energy and decrease the chance of attacks.

BIOME TERRAIN

The terrain in ocean biomes boast all kinds of features. From sandy beaches and coral reefs to bottomless trenches and gloomy caves, there's a huge variety.

SEAFLOOR PLANTS

The seafloor is usually covered with various plants such as seagrass and kelp, which can be gathered and used to craft many handy items.

OCEAN ANIMALS

The surface of frozen ocean biomes is mostly solid ice and fairly barren. Here you'll often encounter rabbits, polar bears and strays spawning.

SHIPWRECKS

You'll also find many shipwrecks and ocean ruins to explore. These can contain loot chests full of goodies, but also be home to deadly mobs.

UNDERWATER MOBS

Underwater mobs such as drowned, guardians and elder guardians can attack swiftly, so keep your eyes open at all times when exploring the ocean depths.

CORAL REEFS

Coral reefs can be the perfect location for creating an amazing underwater base or other large structures for tropical fish to swim around.

PASSIVE MOBS

Many passive mobs inhabit ocean biomes. These can include fish, squid, dolphins, turtles, all of which can be used as food or for crafting.

SWIMMING WITH DOLPHINS

Grab on to a passing dolphin and you'll be able to swim much faster in the water! These aquatic mobs will also find loot for you if you feed them raw fish.

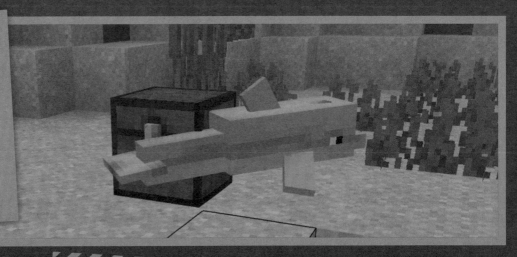

OCEAN MONUMENTS

Ocean monuments are huge underwater structures inhabited by lethal guardians and elder guardians. Unfortunately they don't contain any loot chests at all.

FROZEN BIOMES

The terrain in ocean biomes boast all kinds of features. From sandy beaches and coral reefs to bottomless trenches and gloomy caves, there's a huge variety.

SAIL THE SEVEN SEAS

If you manage to visit all of the ocean biomes in Minecraft on Xbox consoles, you'll earn yourself a very cool Sail the seven seas achievement.

TOP 10 EPIC BUILDS

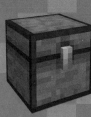

HEROBRINE'S MANSION

The work of Hypixel, this massive mansion is one of the best adventure maps available and is packed with custom enemies, bosses, special items and potions.

PLANET IMPOSSIBLE

Having crash-landed on this barren wasteland, players have to survive for 10 days by exploring the world, finding human settlers and taming a dinosaur!

VERTOAK CITY

When it comes to size and freedom to explore, Vertoak City has it all. The map includes high-rise buildings, sandy beaches and leafy suburbs to discover.

THE DROPPER 2

On this map you have to drop down from an incredible height through a maze of blocks and barriers. Can you make it all the way through to safety?

THE PUZZLE CUBE

This is a Minecraft map with a difference. Players have to walk on the sides of the cube world, solving puzzles as they go to make it to the centre chamber.